CORBEN AND THE CROW COMMUTE

CORBEN
— AND THE —
CROW COMMUTE

EMILY LONIE
ILLUSTRATED BY
AMY KNILL

Corben and the Crow Commute
Copyright © 2023 by Emily Lonie

Gathering Oak Press

No part of this book may be reproduced in whole or in part, stored in a retrieval system or transmitted in any form or by any means, without the prior written permission of the publisher.

Illustrations by Amy Knill
Editing by Naomi Pauls (Paper Trail Publishing)
Type design by Jazmin Welch (fleck creative studio)

ISBN (paperback): 978-1-7390791-0-9

For the Archivists Who Write
(Sylvia, Denise, and Sonia).
Thank you for being Corben's biggest fans.

Contents

11	CHAPTER 1	TOOL SCHOOL
19	CHAPTER 2	CHICK DUTY
27	CHAPTER 3	A CLOSE CALL
35	CHAPTER 4	STEVEN SEAGULL
45	CHAPTER 5	A SECRET GROVE
55	CHAPTER 6	CHATTERBOX
63	CHAPTER 7	AW, NUTS!
75	CHAPTER 8	TO THE RESCUE
85	CHAPTER 9	RITA'S RABBITS
93	CHAPTER 10	DANGER OVERHEAD
101	CHAPTER 11	A VOICE IN THE SKY
109	CHAPTER 12	A NEW LIFE
119		THE REAL CROW COMMUTE

Every day, thousands of crows commute to the big city to provide for their families.

They all enjoy their daily commute.

All except one.

CHAPTER 1
TOOL SCHOOL

The dawn sun peeks over the horizon and glints off the icy-blue glass of the city's tallest tower. Corben Crow stands at the very top with his wings outstretched. He ruffles his tail feathers, revealing a single white feather that stands out against his shiny black body. His powerful talons curl over the edge of the building. He takes a deep breath and dives off the tower. His ecstatic cheers echo between the buildings as he soars towards the ground.

Suddenly, he hears a loud, piercing sound. *CAW, CAW, CAW, CAW.*

The sound wrenches him out of his dream. He opens one eye and sees that his mother, Sheryl, is hovering over him on the tree branch, only an inch from his ear. She is cawing over and over again.

"Do we have to do this every morning?" she asks, poking him with her beak.

Corben opens his other eye and looks around. He realizes that it was all a dream. He isn't jumping off the city's tallest tower. He isn't having an adventure. It's morning. And he's late. Again.

"Leave me alone, Mom," he whines, but Sheryl's pecking becomes more forceful and soon Corben decides to get up. He yawns and stretches his wings. He stands and flexes his talons. He can still feel the wind in his feathers, and he tries to savour his dream for a little bit longer.

"No time for stretching," says Sheryl. "You've already missed the first wave." She fusses with Corben's tail feathers, which are standing up in all directions. Corben has no interest in having his feathers smoothed. He likes them the way they are. He wiggles away so his mother can't reach his tail. He chuckles to himself because he can see that she is ready to explode.

Sheryl grabs Corben with her wings and spins him around to face her.

"Grow up, Corben. Your father pulled a lot of strings to get you into that school. I don't want you to embarrass him by being late again. He has enough on his mind." She sighs and softens her grip on Corben. She lowers her voice. "They were back last night, you know. With signs."

Corben pulls free of his mother and ruffles his feathers so they fall back just the way he likes them. "You don't even know what the signs mean," he says.

Sheryl shakes her head. "Your grandfather said this was how it started last time."

"Chill, Mom. With all this stressing, you'll end up with dull feathers like Auntie Kate."

"You little brat! Take that back!" Sheryl gives Corben a playful shove and he shoots her a cheeky grin.

"Right, mister, get going," she says and shoos him with her wing. "You'll miss the *last* wave if you don't hurry."

"Do I have to? It's so boring."

"Tough grubs, mister. You're not a chick anymore. It's time for you to grow up and start helping the family."

Corben sighs loudly and takes off, joining the thousands of black birds silhouetted against the dawn sky.

Corben dips and dives, trying his best to make the commute more exciting. He flies past crows clutching briefcases and carrying small umbrellas made of sticks and leaves. The commuters chatter away to each other, but Corben has no interest in their small talk.

Soon he spies his teacher and classmates perched on one of the highest branches of a large spruce tree. He sighs to himself and flies down to meet them.

"So nice of you to join us, Corben," says Professor Pluma. He is a wise old bird with a lot of grey feathers around his beak. He stands in front of a large knot in the tree. Next to him is an open briefcase containing a variety of small sticks.

"I wouldn't miss this for the world, Professor. What are we pokin' today?"

Professor Pluma shakes his head slowly and turns his attention to the other young crows on the branch. "As I was saying, today is about choosing the right tool for the job. You need to know how all the different tools are used so you will be ready for any situation."

Reaching into the briefcase, the professor uses his beak to pull out a stick with a curved, hooked end. "When you are dealing with a deep crevice, the best tool to use is the birch hook," he says. "It is best for capturing insects in their larval phase."

Professor Pluma demonstrates a sweeping motion in the knot of the tree. He then holds up the stick to show his three students the wiggling larva stuck to the end. The other crows nod their heads, but all Corben can think of is how delicious the larva looks. He wishes he hadn't skipped breakfast.

"Now, when you need to be precise, the birch won't do," says Professor Pluma. Next, he pulls out a straight, thick stick. "I recommend either maple or beech. You can sharpen the end with your beak to achieve a fine point."

Midway through his demonstration, he notices that Corben is staring off into the distance.

"Corben Crow! Are you listening?" asks Professor Pluma.

"Yep, sure. Maple. Beak. Got it," Corben mutters.

Professor Pluma swaps the sharpened stick for a long blade of grass. "Now, this one takes a bit of getting used to, but it can be an effective item in your tool kit."

Meanwhile, Corben cranes his neck to watch a plane rumbling overhead. Its jet stream makes a puffy white arc against the blue sky. He wonders what it would be like to fly that high. Suddenly, a blade of grass appears in front of his eyes.

"Corben, would you like to show us the grass technique?" asks Professor Pluma.

"Uh … sure," says Corben. He takes the blade of grass in his beak and hops over to a small crevice in a nearby branch. He stabs the blade of grass clumsily into the crevice, but it bends with no effect. The student crows chuckle and click to each other.

Professor Pluma takes the blade of grass from Corben and puts it back in the briefcase. He pats Corben on the back with his wing. "I need you to pay a little more attention, Corben," he says and then turns to the others.

"I think that will be all for today. Please bring your own sticks tomorrow so you can practise the sharpening technique. Don't forget that this exercise will count towards your final mark, so choose wisely."

Corben still has his head in the clouds. Before he realizes the class is over, his fellow students fly off together, leaving him alone on the branch with Professor Pluma. "Corben, please try to take this seriously. I know my lessons may not seem very exciting, but these are critical life skills you're learning here. Your father would want you to…" Professor Pluma can barely get the words out before Corben takes off.

"Yep. My father. Great crow," says Corben as he flies away.

CHAPTER 2
CHICK DUTY

Corben is on his way home when suddenly—*thwack!* He is knocked out of the sky and lands on the ground with a *thump*. He looks around frantically, afraid that an eagle is about to attack him. But instead of an eagle, he hears the cackling caws of two crows. His best friends, brothers Russell and Cameron, perch on the power line above him. Their feathers are pushed up into the centre of their heads in the crow version of a punk hairdo.

"You bailed so hard!" says Russell.

"We got you, Corb," chuckles Cameron.

Corben sneers at them and then bursts out laughing. He flies up to join his buddies on the power line. "I thought it was an eagle. My whole life flashed before my eyes."

"Musta' been short," says Cameron.

"Yeah, and dull," replies Corben.

"That's because you're always in school. You need to hang out with us more," says Russell.

"I don't think my father would approve of me spending more time with you guys," says Corben.

"He's so lame," says Cameron.

Russell puffs out his chest and struts along the power line doing an impression of Corben's father. "I'm Mayor Crow. I'm super important and no one is allowed to have any fun."

Cameron and Russell burst out laughing. Corben hesitates for a moment but then he laughs along with them.

A woman walking along the sidewalk looks up at the cackling crows on the power line. Corben notices her below and he puts the tip of his wing up to his beak, telling Russell and Cameron to be quiet. "I'll show you fun," he whispers.

Corben hovers his back end over the power line and lets go a stream of silvery blue poop. It lands on the woman's head with a *plop*. She screams and locks eyes with Corben. He caws loudly and she jumps and runs away, wiping the poop from her hair.

"Works every time," says Corben. Russell and Cameron cackle and each give Corben a thumbs-up with the tip of one wing—two wingtips-up.

The three birds spend the afternoon watching the bustle of city life around them. Humans walk down the sidewalk in fancy suits. Colourful cars flash past on the road. The traffic gets busier and busier as the humans start their own evening commute. As the sun begins to fade, Corben spots the commuting crows returning home for the night. The sky fills with raucous cawing and suddenly hundreds of crows are perched on every available inch of the power lines.

"I guess I should go. My mom will be expecting me with the commute," says Corben. "My dad would be really mad if I missed dinner." Corben ruffles his wings and prepares to take off. "See you guys later?" he asks.

"Hope the old crow lets you out," says Russell.

Corben takes off and joins the commute, waving to his friends as he disappears among the sea of black feathers in the sky.

Corben lands softly in his family's tree and tiptoes around, trying not to be heard. A twig snaps under his foot. So much for being quiet.

"I hear you, Corben. Come down here, please."

Corben sighs and jumps off the branch, landing close to his father. With his jet-black feathers and large wingspan, Carlos is a commanding presence. "I need you to watch the chicks tonight while your mother and I go to the community meeting."

"But Russ and Cam are going—"

"I don't care what your good-for-nothing friends are up to," says Carlos. "We need you here to protect the nest."

"But Dad—"

"Enough!" Carlos booms. Corben shies away and flops down with a huff. He knows he shouldn't argue when his dad gets like this. "We will be back after the meeting. We are trusting you to keep the chicks safe." Carlos stares at Corben until he responds.

"Fine," says Corben.

Carlos and Sheryl take off into the evening sky. Corben hops over to the nest. The chicks jump up and down, excited to be with their big brother, but Corben just feels annoyed. After a few minutes, he hears a rustling above him. He looks up and sees Russell and Cameron staring down at him.

"Chick duty?" asks Russell.

"Too bad you're busy," says Cameron. "We're going to the community centre."

"It's your favourite class," says Russell, trying to tempt his friend.

Corben looks at the chicks and then back at Russell and Cameron. He is torn for a moment, but then he makes a decision. He hops over to a branch full of leaves and breaks it off with his beak. He carries the branch over to the nest and places it on top. The chicks squeak and cheep from below the leafy branch.

"Shush!" says Corben. "You'll be fine."

"Genius! Let's go. The class will be over soon," says Cameron.

CHAPTER 3
TROUBLING TIMES

Hundreds of crows line the branches of the Gathering Oak. Their nervous chattering fills the air. Carlos lands on the ground beneath the tree and the crows fall silent. All eyes are on Carlos.

"My fellow crows, our community is in danger," he says in a solemn tone. "The humans have put up signs." A wave of whispers moves through the tree.

"What do they mean?" asks one of the crows.

"We can't know for sure, but the elders have told me stories of the great move all those years ago," says Carlos. He pauses, not sure if he should tell the crows the truth. "It began with signs," he says after a few moments.

"You can't possibly mean…," says one crow.

"But this is our home!" says another.

"My friends, these are troubling times. I need you to prepare yourselves. We may need to find a new roost," says Carlos sadly.

"Mayor Crow, where would we go?" asks a crow in the crowd.

"I have my scouts on it. In the meantime, please report any unusual activity and as always, keep an eye out for eagles," says Carlos. "While we are focused on this new threat, our enemy may still appear at any time."

Sheryl hops next to Carlos and he wraps his wing around her. "Protect your families. We are all in this together."

A dark shadow looms above the Gathering Oak. Carlos looks up and spots the outline of an eagle circling above. He shivers and gathers Sheryl close to him.

Corben and his friends are perched in a tall fir tree, watching as a young woman walks out of the community centre into the parking lot. She wears a flowy black shirt and stretchy yoga pants and carries a rolled mat under her arm. Her hair is pulled back into a tight ponytail that bounces as she walks. With her cellphone glued to her ear, she talks loudly to a friend on the other end of the line.

Russell looks at Cameron and then at Corben with a mischievous grin. "Ready?" he asks. Corben and Cameron nod. "Now!" yells Russell.

The three crows dive-bomb the woman. They grab at her ponytail and then they swoop back up into the sky. The woman shrieks and flails her arms. She drops her phone and fumbles for her keys in her pocket. The crows swoop down again, flying only inches from her head. She runs for her car, jumps in, and sits for a moment, catching her breath. From inside the car, she can see her cellphone on the ground a few feet away. The screen is cracked.

"Becky? Hello? Are you there?" says the voice in the phone.

The three crow friends regroup in the tree. "Did you see her face?" asks Corben and they fall over laughing.

"Thanks, guys," says Corben once he composes himself. "I needed that tonight. My dad is being super annoying lately. He's all, 'Corben grow up. Stop having fun.' "

"Our dad's like that too," says Cameron.

"What's so wrong with having fun?" asks Corben. "What's so great about being a grown-up anyway? My dad never seems very happy."

Russell and Cameron shrug. "Beats me," says Cameron.

Corben notices that the moon has risen in the sky. "I should probably go. I'll be a dead bird if my parents get home and I'm not there. See you guys tomorrow."

Cruising back to his family's tree, Corben chuckles to himself about the yoga lady prank. But as he approaches his tree, he stops laughing. Something is wrong. There are leaves and broken branches scattered everywhere. Carlos is pacing back and forth and there is a deep red cut across his face. Corben dives down and lands next to his mother. She is rocking the smallest chick back and forth. His little wing is broken, and he is cheeping faintly as Sheryl cradles him in her wings.

 Carlos flies at Corben and pins him up against the trunk of the tree with his powerful wing. "You selfish little brat!" he yells. "How could you? They were helpless! The eagle could have killed them if we hadn't come home in time."

 "Dad, I...," stutters Corben.

 "I've been trying to teach you to be a responsible member of this family, but you insist on disobeying me," says Carlos. "Now look what you've done."

"I was only gone for a bit. I thought it would be fine," says Corben.

"That's the problem. You only think about yourself. You think life is all fun and games, but your actions have consequences, Corben!"

"Well, *this* isn't fun," says Corben, under his breath.

"Grow up, Corben," says Carlos, releasing his grasp. "It's time you acted your age."

"Why? So I can be boring and mean like you are all the time?" Corben yells. "So I can pretend I'm so important and better than everyone? I don't want to be like you."

"I hate to break it to you, son, but this is life. We all have a role to play. The community depends on me. The sooner you grow up and stop being such a brat, the better." Carlos turns away. "I can't even look at you right now."

"But Dad…," says Corben.

"No. Get out of my sight," says Carlos.

"FINE!" yells Corben. "I don't need this. I don't need to be on chick duty all the time. I don't need your stupid school. I don't need you always yelling at me and telling me to grow up. I don't need any of it and I don't need you!"

Corben flies off into the night. He refuses to look back.

CHAPTER 4
STEVEN SEAGULL

In the early dawn light, a sleepy Corben roosts in a spindly tree in the middle of the city sidewalk. He is alone except for a jogger passing by. He hears cawing in the distance. Looking up, he sees the first wave of the crow commute flying into the city. His first instinct is to join them but then he scowls and turns his back on the commuting crows.

He hops out of his tiny tree and hides behind a garbage can so the crows won't see him. From here, Corben watches the city come to life. A van pulls up and a man in a baseball cap jumps out with a pile of newspapers. He opens the metal box next to the garbage can and plunks the newspapers inside. *Bang!* The spring-loaded door slams shut, making Corben jump.

A woman in a blue skirt and high heels hurries down the sidewalk with a coffee cup in her hand. She takes a big sip and then throws the cup towards the garbage can. But she misses and the brown liquid drips down the side of the can, right onto Corben's head. He scowls and wipes the coffee off of his beak with his wing. Then he hops out from his hiding spot and lunges at the woman with a loud *CAW!* She jumps and scurries down the sidewalk. For a moment, Corben forgets about his anger and laughs.

Soon, the only thing he can think about is breakfast. His stomach grumbles loudly and he cradles it with his wing. He really wants to eat some grubs, but he can't see any grass. He hops up onto the top of the garbage can. Inside he sees a banana peel, a half-eaten baloney sandwich, and an apple core. He grabs the apple core in his beak and jumps back down to the ground. He has only taken one bite when he hears a voice.

"M'boy, there is a simpler way, with more exciting results," says the voice.

Corben drops his apple core. He looks left. He looks right. But he can't see a body to go with the strange voice. Then he hears a *tap-tap-tapping* above his head. A giant seagull is staring down at him from the top of the garbage can.

"While we all indulge in the odd bit of dumpster food from time to time, those among us with fancier tastes have found a better way to satisfy our cravings," says the large white bird.

"Huh?" says Corben.

"Oh, my dear boy, forgive me. I do tend to use big words," says the seagull and then he bows. "Steven Seagull, at your service. Follow me for better food."

Corben looks at the strange bird towering over him and then at the tiny brown apple core

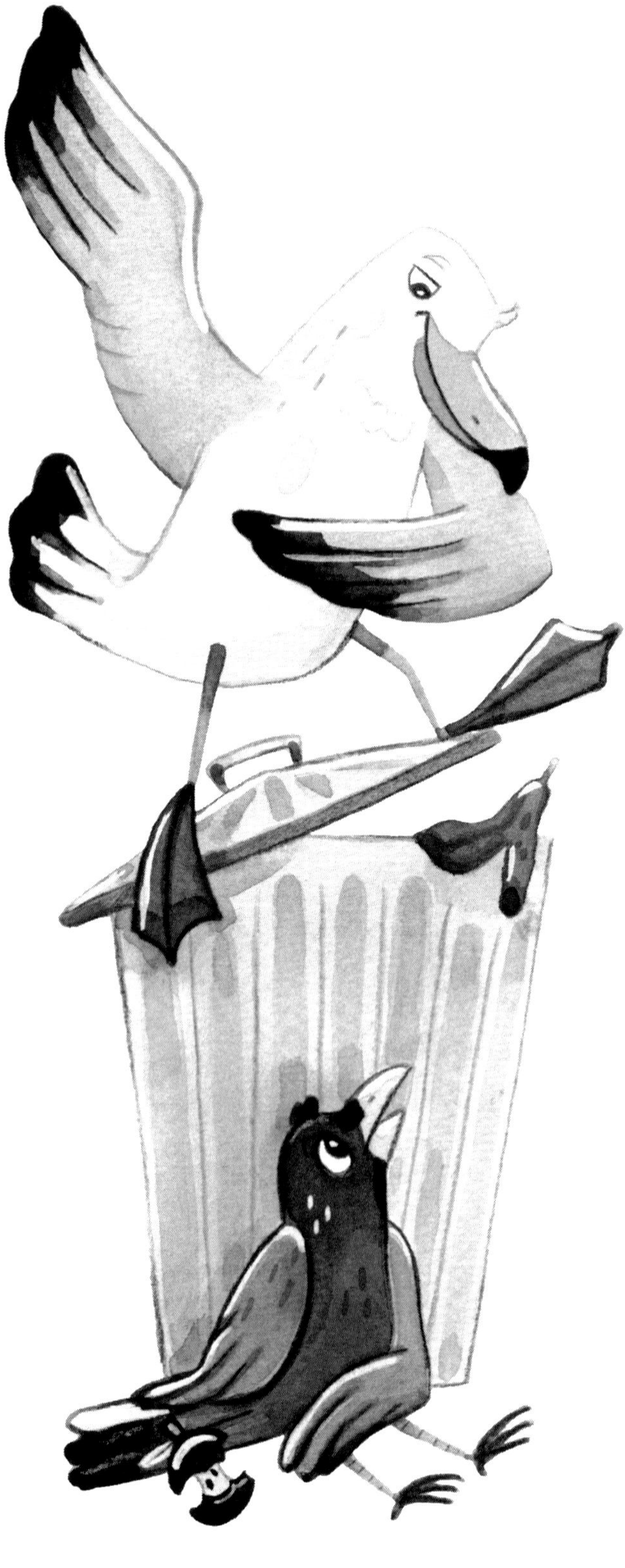

on the ground in front of him. Maybe this bird might know how to find better food. He decides it's worth a shot.

"Hi Steven. I'm Corben. I'm pretty hungry."

Steven and Corben drift on the wind towards the ocean. Then Steven slows and hovers over a big market filled with humans and delicious food smells. Steven spots a group of children standing together a few feet away from their parents. One small boy holds a paper container filled with golden French fries.

"Welcome to Granville Island," Steven says to Corben. "Let's eat!"

Steven lands behind a bench and Corben follows him. The two birds huddle beneath the bench, watching the children.

"The key is to avoid the large humans," says Steven. "Wait here. Let me demonstrate." Steven creeps towards the boy with the french fries. When he gets close, he lets out a mighty *SQUAWK*. The little boy leaps in the air and lets go of his container of fries. Steven grabs it in his beak and hops back under the bench.

Corben and Steven eagerly munch on the crunchy fries and the grease drips down their beaks. Between mouthfuls, Steven says, "That may have looked easy, young crow, but you must be careful. They must never see you coming and you must always watch out for their feet. One swift kick could cost you."

When the fries are gone, Steven motions his head towards a little girl holding a waffle cone filled with rainbow ice cream. "Now it's your turn," he says. "I believe a spot of dessert may be in order."

Corben grins and nods his head. He checks to make sure the bigger humans are distracted. He hops towards the girl, just like Steven did. So far, so good. But then Corben gets too excited and decides to try out a new method. He flaps his wings and jumps onto the girl's head. She screams and throws her ice cream into the air. It lands on the ground with a gooey *smack*.

"Mummy!" she screams. "The bird landed ON MY HEAD!" She waves her arms around in panic and hits Corben. He lands on the ground with a *thump* that knocks him out. Steven scrambles from under the bench and pokes Corben with his beak. "We must go, m'boy," he says. "You made a mess of that." Corben wakes up to see the little girl crying and a group of angry humans staring at him.

"Fly!" cries Steven. Corben takes off just in the nick of time as a large foot narrowly misses his tail. Steven and Corben fly as hard as they can and land on the roof of a building at the other end of the island.

"That was close," says Corben.

"Indeed," says Steven. "A touch too close for my taste. Let's try for an easier meal next time."

"That place was pretty cool though," says Corben. "Could you show me some more of your favourite spots?"

"I would be delighted to be your tour guide, m'boy," says Steven.

The pair spend the day visiting all of Steven's favourite places along the waterfront. Corben soars through the air, feeling the wind in his feathers. He has never felt this free before. His dad never lets him go beyond the commuting route.

After a full day of flying, Corben starts to feel hungry again. "Hey Steven, how about some dinner?" he asks.

"That sounds grand. I know just the place," replies Steven.

CHAPTER 5
A SECRET GROVE

Steven and Corben land on the rigging of a fishing trawler tied up in bustling Steveston Harbour. Colourful boats line the docks, their long metal fishing poles sticking out in every direction. Seagulls circle overhead, waiting to dive down to pick up scraps of fish. Corben has never seen anything like it. He stares in amazement and grins.

"This is so cool!" says Corben.

"Indeed. A truly magical place," says Steven. He is pleased that Corben is so taken with the harbour. He points to a nearby trawler with his wing. "That, m'boy, is the *Salty Sea*. A fine vessel with an able captain, who just so happens to be a friend of mine."

Steven and Corben fly over to the *Salty Sea* and land on the dock nearby. The Captain is a burly man dressed in black rubber waders and a bright yellow hat. He is standing on the stern of the boat, gutting a silvery fish with a metal cleaver. With one smooth chopping motion, he lops off the head with a loud *thud*.

Steven squawks at the Captain to get his attention. "Well, lookie here," says the Captain. "Where've you been?

Not like you to miss a meal." He notices Corben. "And I see you've brought a friend. I suppose you'll be expectin' a second portion today?"

Steven nods his head enthusiastically. The Captain reaches into a big blue bucket on the deck of the boat and pulls out two large fish heads. He tosses them to the birds on the dock. Steven stands at attention and salutes the fisherman with his wing. The Captain tips his hat in response.

"Now don't forget, we'll be headin' out to sea tomorrow, bright and early. Don't be late," says the Captain.

Steven squawks in response. Then he and Corben collect their fish heads and fly over to the big iron gate at the entrance to the harbour. Perched on top of the gate, they tear meaty chunks of fish from the bones. They smile at each other as they munch on their fishy feast.

Soon enough, the sun begins to set. In the distance, Corben can see the first wave of the crow commute heading for home. Steven notices Corben looking off into the distance.

"It's getting late," says Steven. "I suppose you'll be needing to join your family on the commute. It was lovely to meet you, Corben. I have truly enjoyed my day with you, m'boy."

Corben looks down and picks at the remaining bits of fish head. "I'm not going home," he says.

Steven can sense that Corben is upset and he tries to reassure his new friend. "Oh, I see. Well then, fancy roosting with me tonight?" he asks. "You would be most welcome."

Corben looks up at Steven and smiles. "Thanks. That would be really cool."

"Not a problem, m'boy," replies Steven. "Follow me."

Corben and Steven soar along the coast, heading north towards the towering blue mountains. They are two silhouettes against the evening sky, but all of a sudden, a third silhouette appears.

A big one. Corben doesn't notice the danger until it's almost too late.

"Eagle!" yells Steven. Corben turns around just as the eagle swoops down with his sharp talons outstretched, in attack mode. Steven and Corben fly in opposite directions, trying to get away. The eagle follows Corben, the easier prey. Corben dives and swoops, desperate to escape. He sets his sights on the tall towers ahead.

When he reaches the city, Corben flies between the buildings and then swoops down to hover near the ground.

He alternates this pattern, trying to dodge his attacker. The eagle is so focused on Corben that he doesn't see Steven coming up on his flank. Steven flies straight into him, knocking him off his flight path. The eagle falls to the ground with a hard *smack*.

Corben looks back to see the dazed eagle picking himself up off the pavement. He lets out a furious *screech* that echoes off the buildings.

"We'd best get moving, young crow," says Steven. "That was Edgar. I've had a run-in with him before and he is not to be trifled with. We'll be safe once we reach the grove."

Carlos is standing on a branch of the family's tree with his wing around Sheryl. They are speaking to a crow wearing a pinecone hat and a badge made from leaves.

"When did you last see your son?" asks Constable Crow.

"Last night," says Sheryl.

"Can you describe him for me?"

"He has a white tail feather and he…," Sheryl trails off. "My poor boy. He's out there all alone."

"Is there any reason he might have flown off?"

Sheryl and Carlos exchange looks. "There was … an incident and I … I was harsh with him," says Carlos. "I said some things I didn't mean."

"We find that with family arguments, some birds just need a little time to cool off. I am sure your son will be back soon. In the meantime, I'll file a report. Let me know if you hear anything from him in the next twenty-four hours."

"Thank you, Constable," says Sheryl.

"You're welcome, ma'am." Constable Crow tips his hat and flies away.

"Our son is missing and all he can say is he'll file a report?" says Carlos.

"What if something happened to him?" asks Sheryl with tears in her eyes.

"I'll find him," says Carlos. "I promise."

CORBEN AND THE CROW COMMUTE

"I thought we were going to a grove," says Corben. He and Steven are standing on the forest floor in front of a giant rock wall covered in green moss. Steven hops over to the base of the wall and pushes aside some of the moss with his wing to reveal a small tunnel.

"Through here, m'boy," says Steven.

The tunnel looks dark and scary. Corben hesitates, but then he hears the screech of an eagle in the distance. Without delay, he hops forward to follow Steven into the tunnel. After a few minutes in the dark, the two birds emerge into an expansive grove that is protected on all sides by towering old-growth fir trees.

"Welcome to my home," says Steven. "You'll be safe here."

"Wow, it's huge. You live here all alone?" asks Corben. "You don't have a roosting community?"

"When I was a chick, I fell out of my nest and broke my leg. I couldn't fly so my parents abandoned me," says Steven. "Fortunately, I was rescued by a human called Nigel, who fixed my broken leg and raised me with his family. Once I got big and strong, he found this place for me where I would be safe."

"It's so cool that you get to live alone, with no one telling you what to do," says Corben.

"The grove is lovely, that is true, but it's not all it's cracked up to be, m'boy. It can get pretty lonely, and I have to make sure I have enough food to eat. It was difficult after Nigel left me here. I didn't know how to get food for myself. I had no other seagulls to teach me how to survive."

"What did you do?" asks Corben.

"I scavenged in garbage cans for a while, just as you were doing this morning, but then I found the Captain and we became partners. Now I go out to sea with him and I clean up all the fishy parts that the humans don't want. Humans are very picky creatures."

Steven hops over to a pile of moss on the forest floor. He jumps into it and settles himself down for the night. Corben looks around and picks a comfy-looking branch where he can roost.

"I'll be heading out to sea in the morning and I'll be gone for a few days," says Steven, "but you're welcome to stay here as long as you like. Good night, young crow."

"G'night, Steven," says Corben and closes his eyes. He is asleep almost instantly.

CHAPTER 6
CHATTERBOX

Corben wakes in the morning and finds himself alone in the big grove. On a normal day, his mom would have woken him up at dawn, but today the sun is already high in the sky. Usually, he would be at tool school by now, but instead he has the whole day to himself. He knows just what to do.

Corben stands at the very top of the magnificent Lions Gate Bridge. He looks around at the city in the distance, like he is king of the world. Smiling, he stretches his wings wide, flexes his talons, and plummets from the bridge with an excited *screech*. Just before he hits the water, he changes course and skims along the surface. The salty spray dampens his feathers as he glides.

Ahead he sees the majestic trees of Stanley Park. He flaps his wings and flies to the top of one of the tallest trees—a giant Douglas fir. When he lands, he spots a grey squirrel a few branches below. It is bounding towards him—fast. The squirrel leaps at Corben, nearly knocking him off the branch.

"That was amazing! I can't believe you jumped off the bridge like that. I've always wanted to do that, but of course I don't have any wings so that would be super dangerous. But you can fly, and you did, and it looked awesome!" chatters the squirrel, talking a mile a minute.

Corben is confused. He doesn't quite have time to make sense of it all before the squirrel is off again.

"I've always wanted to fly. Ever since I was a little kitten, my mom always said I was meant to be a flying squirrel, but I was born into the wrong species. But I make up for it in enthusiasm and speed and I'm really fast. Wanna race?" She stands back on her hind legs in anticipation, waiting for a reply. Her body quivers, ready to move at any moment. Corben takes too long to answer and she starts chattering again.

"Oh no, I forgot my manners. My mom would have scolded me for that. I forgot to introduce myself and I went straight into a challenge, how rude of me. My name is Sadie." She pauses just long enough for Corben to introduce himself.

"I'm Corben. Did you say something about a race?"

"First one to the ground wins. GO!" yells Sadie. She leaps into the air and disappears. Corben jumps off the branch, slaps his wings to his sides, and rockets after her. Sadie leaps between the trees, jumping from branch to branch. She is fast but Corben is faster. He lands on the ground with a few seconds to spare. When Sadie arrives, Corben struts around in a circle, showing off.

"I win, I win, I win," he says.

"I wish I had wings. That looked awesome. That was such a good race. I just love that feeling of jumping into the air, almost feels like flying or what I guess flying would feel like. You're so lucky that you can fly. It must be so much fun," says Sadie.

"I've never really thought about it that way. It's just something I do. But I guess it's pretty cool," says Corben.

"Oh-oh-oh-oh-oh!" says Sadie as she jumps up and down on the spot. "I'm no match for you on the way down, but what about up?"

Corben extends his wings, ready to fly. "You're on," he says.

"Wait-wait-wait! Obviously you have the advantage again, so I think we need to change the rules to make it fair. I think you should have to get to the top like I do, yeah, that's good. If I can't fly, neither can you," says Sadie.

"Okay, no flying," says Corben.

"No flying and … no wings!" says Sadie. "On your marks, get set, GO!"

Sadie has a head start again. Corben flaps his wings once but then remembers the rules and tucks them behind his back. He hops over to the base of the tree and stares upwards. The nearest branch is too far away for him to jump. Sadie is vanishing quickly as she scrambles up the trunk of the tree. She stops briefly and looks down at Corben on the ground.

"Hurry up, slowpoke. Just because you don't have your wings doesn't mean you can't climb," she says.

Corben sighs. He jumps into the air and grabs hold of the trunk with his talons. He starts to fall backwards but then he grabs the bark with his beak. He lets go with one foot and reaches it up, sinking his talons into the bark. Then he grabs hold with his other foot and then his beak again. He starts to pick up a rhythm, like a mountain climber finding his groove. Soon he is gaining on Sadie but with such a head start, she reaches the top first. She runs around pumping her little paws in the air to celebrate her win.

Corben isn't far behind and soon enough, he hops onto the top branch and flexes his wings. "I definitely prefer flying but that was pretty cool. I didn't know I could climb like that," he says.

"Welcome to squirrel world, Corben. There's climbing and jumping and leaping," says Sadie.

"Can you show me more of squirrel world?" asks Corben.

"Oh boy, oh boy, oh boy, you bet. What should we do first? Oh! I'll take you to my favourite place, it's so much fun!" Sadie leaps into the air and lands in the next tree. In an instant, she is in the next tree and then the next. Corben follows her through the forest, wondering where this energetic little squirrel is taking him.

CHAPTER 7
AW, NUTS!

Corben lands next to Sadie on top of a long wooden fence. There are bright blue pools inside the fence and lots of humans walking around. He can hear music and the excited shrieks of small children. A voice interrupts the music. "Good afternoon, folks. Start making your way to the Wild Coast. The next show will begin in fifteen minutes."

"What *is* this place?" asks Corben.

"An ocean of wonders, Corben. Come on, come on, come on." Sadie jumps off the fence and Corben loses sight of her. He searches for a sign of her puffy grey tail. Soon he spots her. He flies over and lands next to Sadie on a wet rock beside a small pool. His feet make a satisfying splash as he lands, and he jumps up and down a few times. Sadie copies him and the two of them jump up and down, laughing as they splash.

Suddenly, Corben is drenched by a wave of water. He shakes his feathers and looks up to see a furry brown face with long white whiskers. The face is attached to a long sleek body. Corben has never seen anything like this creature. He backs away, but Sadie smiles. "Don't worry, the otters are very friendly. This is Olivia."

Olivia dives backwards into the pool and instantly resurfaces, splashing Corben a second time. She slides onto the slippery rock on her belly and rests her chin in her paws, looking at Corben.

AW, NUTS!

"And who might you be?" asks Olivia. Before Corben can answer, she jumps back into the pool and then back up onto the rock in a flash. "What's the matter? Cat got your tongue? My goodness, that would be a sight to see, wouldn't it?"

"I'm Corb—" Before Corben can finish saying his name, Olivia slides back into the water. She resurfaces with a ball on her chest and spins around, holding the ball. She seems to have completely forgotten about Corben. Another otter appears, poking her head out of the water.

"Forgive my silly friend. She's had too many sugary treats today," says the second otter. She rubs the fur on her face with her paws. "I'm Orra. What brings you down to earth, my feathered friend?"

"Orra, this is Corben. We met in the tree and we had a race and it was awesome. But he wanted me to show him squirrel world, so of course I brought him here to introduce him to you two and to see the show. Ah, the show! It's going to start soon so we should go-go-go," chatters Sadie.

"Before you go-go-go, little Sadie, make sure to watch out for old Bill. You know he has his eye on you," says Orra.

"Don't worry, I'm way too fast for that big oaf. He's never been able to catch—" The loudspeaker interrupts Sadie.

"Get ready, folks. The two o'clock show is about to begin."

Humans of all ages are gathered around a large, crystal-blue pool. They buzz with excitement as they watch the glassy surface of the water. Corben and Sadie are perched on the wooden fence, ready for the show.

Suddenly, a silky-smooth dolphin pierces the water's surface and flies into the air. The crowd gasps. The graceful creature makes a perfect arc ten feet above the pool and then crashes down into the water. A wave splashes over the railing and soaks the humans in the first row. They scream in surprise and then howl with laughter.

"That's how we say hello here at the Vancouver Aquarium," says a woman in a red shirt, standing beside the pool. "Welcome, everyone! You've just met Delilah, our Pacific white-sided dolphin."

Delilah's back and dorsal fin are dark grey and her chin, throat, and belly are creamy white. She jumps into the air again and falls backwards, splashing into the water. When she comes back to the surface, the woman in red throws her a fish. Delilah screeches in response and throws the fish up into the air before gobbling it down.

"Delilah has lived with us here at the Vancouver Aquarium for five years. She was found tangled in a fishing net off the coast of British Columbia and brought to the aquarium to get better." The woman in red blows a high-pitched whistle and Delilah appears at the surface of the pool. She rolls onto her side to reveal her right flipper.

"As you can see, folks, Delilah's right flipper was injured by the fishing net. We realized that she wouldn't be able to swim fast enough to catch fish in the wild, so now she lives here." The woman blows her whistle again and Delilah sinks below the surface. She is gone for only a second before she leaps out of the water again. The crowd cheers and claps.

Delilah waves her flippers and screeches, "Hi, Sadie!"

Sadie grins and waves her paw at Delilah. She turns to Corben. "Isn't she great? She loves to put on a show but she always says hi to me. She always finds a way to work it into her performance 'cause she's such a pro."

Corben claps his wings together, loving the show, but then his stomach starts to grumble.

"Sorry to interrupt, but do you think we could find some food?" he asks. "It's been a while since I ate."

"Sure, let's find some grub," says Sadie.

"Some grubs would be nice," says Corben.

"Eww," says Sadie. "I have something much better in mind, come on, come on, come on. They have the best roasted nuts at the snack stand and sometimes the humans drop them. Hurry, hurry, hurry!" Sadie bounds away and Corben rushes after her.

Corben and Sadie are hiding under a bush staring longingly at the aquarium's snack stand. They watch as a customer approaches. Sadie's eyes light up when she hears him order a bag of the mixed nuts, but her excitement quickly fades as she hears the cashier say, "Sorry, we're sold out."

Corben can see that Sadie is disappointed. He looks around the snack area. Sitting next to one of the big blue pools is a small boy, holding a bag of nuts. Corben knows what he has to do.

"Don't worry, Sadie. I'll get us those nuts." He feels confident about trying Steven's snack-getting technique. He tiptoes from under the bush and hops ever so slowly towards the small boy.

Meanwhile, a human with a bushy moustache and a big belly emerges from the maintenance shed near the fence. He wears a dark blue uniform, with the name BILL sewn on his chest in bold letters. Hanging from his belt is a walkie-talkie, a small green net, and a large brass key ring that jangles as he walks.

Sadie sees Bill and she panics. She waves her little paws in the air and squeals, trying to get her new friend's attention. "Corben, Corben, Corben, look over here, look over here. Why aren't you looking over here? Watch out, Bill's coming!" It's no use. Corben doesn't hear her.

The little boy is crunching away on his delicious nutty snack. Corben sneaks up behind him and lets out a mighty *CAW!* The noise makes everyone jump, including the little boy. He drops the bag as expected, but Corben is not prepared for what comes next.

The boy starts screaming and then the ground begins to shake. Corben looks up just in time to see a green net swooping towards him. He ducks and hops backwards and the net just misses him.

From the other side of the snack stand, Sadie lets out a loud chattering sound, and then she bounds towards Bill. Reaching him, she runs figure eight patterns between his legs.

Sadie's diversion gives Corben enough time to take off. His wings pump as he escapes up and up. Once he reaches a safe height, he turns around and sees that Sadie has distracted the security guard. Landing on a nearby branch, Corben breathes a sigh of relief.

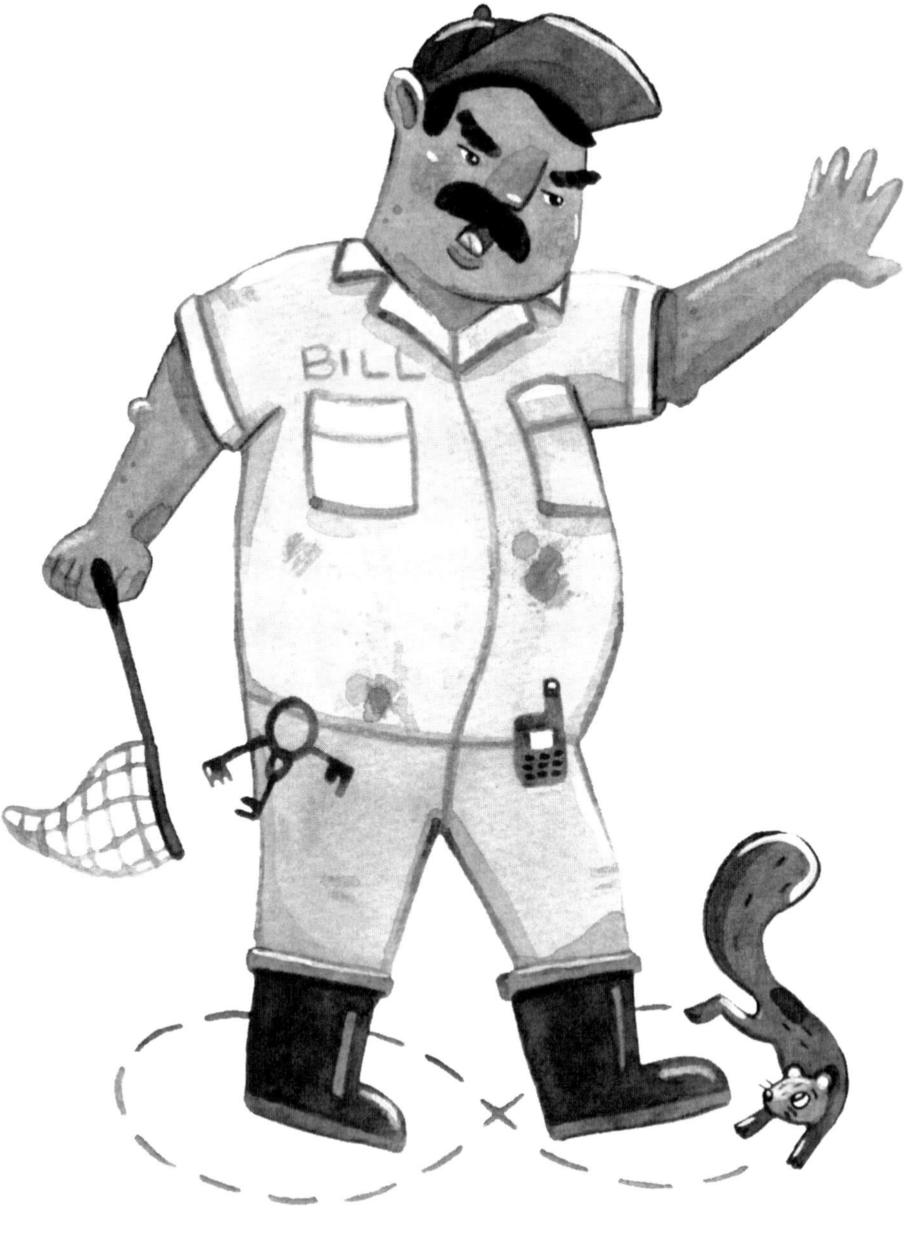
BILL

Sadie looks up at the tree and sees that Corben is safe. She runs back to the cover of the bushes near the snack stand. She hops up onto a rock and is just about to leap onto the fence when the green nylon net comes down on top of her. She jumps and pushes with all her might, trying to escape, but it's no use. Sadie is trapped. She squeals in fear.

"Thought you could get away from me," says Bill, "but I finally got you, you nut stealin' chatter mouse." He picks up the squirrel-filled net and turns to face the crowd that has gathered behind him. "Nothin' to see here, folks. This little devil won't be botherin' you anymore."

CHAPTER 8
TO THE RESCUE

Corben paces on his branch, looking towards the aquarium. He saw what happened, but Sadie and Bill have now vanished from sight. Corben throws up his wings in frustration and takes off.

It wasn't like it was *my* fault, he thinks. She was the one who suggested the nuts.

As he flies farther and farther away, the aquarium becomes smaller and smaller. His mind is a flurry of thoughts and questions. Orra warned her, he thinks. Sadie should have been more careful.

He flaps his wings hard, propelling himself away from the aquarium.

"What could *I* possibly do?" he says out loud. But as he flies farther away, he slows the flapping of his wings. He starts to feel like maybe there *is* something he could do.

I guess Orra might know where Bill is keeping Sadie, he thinks. He flies in a big arc to turn around and he heads back towards the aquarium. "I'm coming, Sadie."

Corben lands on the rock next to the otter pool. "Orra? Olivia?" he calls. Two furry faces pop to the surface of the water. They look at each other and then disappear. "Wait! I need your help!"

The two otters slide out of the water onto the rock and surround Corben.

"Well, hello, feathered friend. Back so soon?" asks Olivia.

"Sadie's been captured!" says Corben.

"Oh no! I knew Bill was going to catch up to her one day. Poor Sadie," says Orra.

"Do you know where he might have taken her?" asks Corben.

"I can only assume he's eaten her by now. Have you seen the size of him?" says Olivia.

"Olivia!" says Orra. "That's not what the humans do." Orra turns to Corben. "I bet he has her in that little den of his. Over there." Orra points her paw at the maintenance shed.

Corben takes off in a flash.

Olivia shakes her furry head. "What a strange creature," she says and then dives backwards into the pool.

Corben stands on the roof of the maintenance shed. He hears the jangling of keys as Bill opens the door and steps out into the sunshine. The door closes behind him but luckily for Corben, it doesn't latch. Bill looks around the aquarium, surveying the various pools. Then he heads towards the dolphin exhibit at the other end of the complex.

Corben hops onto the ground and pushes the door with his beak. After a few tries, he manages to squeeze his head between the door and the frame.

"Sadie?" He hears a squeal from the far end of the shed. He pushes with all his might to move the door enough to get his body through the crack and he hops forward. Then he spins around and sticks his beak out to stop the door from latching. It's dark inside the shed, but he can just make out a large metal cage in the corner.

Sadie jumps up and down, so happy to see him. "You came back for me, thank you, thank you, thank you," she squeals. "But it's no use, the cage is locked and I'm trapped."

Corben examines the latch on the cage. He tries pulling at it with his beak, but nothing happens. He pulls and pushes, but the latch won't budge. He backs away with a huff and slumps down on the floor.

TO THE RESCUE

"It's impossible, Sadie. I don't know what to—" Corben stares off into the distance. After a moment, he turns for the door and speed-hops towards it.

"Wait, Corben. Please don't leave me here. I'm scared," says Sadie.

"I'll be back, I promise." Corben squeezes through the door and leaves it unlatched. He takes off into the sky.

Corben scans the trees below. Pine? he thinks. No. That wasn't it. Cedar? Spruce? No, no, no. Finally, Corben spots a large grove of trees with wide green leaves.

"Maple!" he shouts. He lands in a gigantic maple tree and hops around until he spots the perfect branch. Using his beak, he clamps onto it and breaks it off with a *snap*. He thinks about Professor Pluma's lesson as he sharpens the stick with his beak.

Back in the shed, Corben inserts the sharpened stick into the latch on Sadie's cage. He jostles it, trying to find just the right spot.

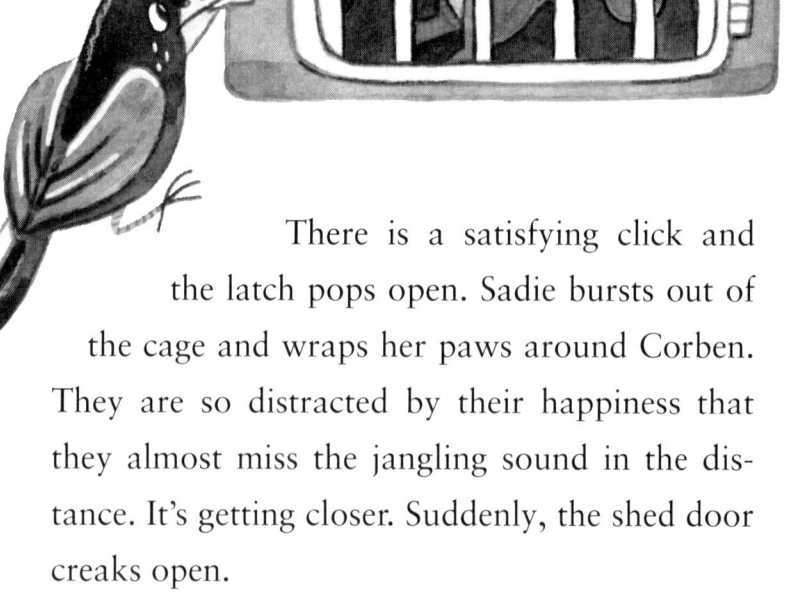

There is a satisfying click and the latch pops open. Sadie bursts out of the cage and wraps her paws around Corben. They are so distracted by their happiness that they almost miss the jangling sound in the distance. It's getting closer. Suddenly, the shed door creaks open.

"Bill!" squeals Sadie. Corben and Sadie look at the door and look back at each other. They are trapped!

"Corben! This way!" Sadie scampers onto the workbench and leaps towards a small window near the roof. She just catches the edge of the windowsill with her paws and hauls herself up onto the ledge. Pushing with all the squirrely strength she can muster, she opens the window a crack, space enough for Corben to fly out. Sadie jumps through the window and lands on the ground. She skitters up the side of the shed and stands on the roof.

Bill runs out of the shed and looks up at Sadie. She sticks out her tongue at him before leaping off the roof onto the closest tree branch. Bill stands bewildered. He can't quite believe his eyes. I was *sure* I locked that cage, he thinks.

"Squirrel world was way more intense than I expected," says Corben. He is perched next to

Sadie on a tree branch, gazing out over the sparkling waters of English Bay.

"I don't know what I would have done without you today," says Sadie. "I really thought I was a goner, but you were there for me. I've never had anyone in my life like that before."

"Don't you have a family?" asks Corben.

"After my mom taught me to jump and climb and find food, she told me it was time for me to go and I've been on my own ever since. Squirrel world can be pretty lonely. Sometimes I dream about what it would be like to have a big family like yours. I see all of you flying together. It must be so nice."

"No way!" says Corben. "The other crows are always meddling in your business and telling you how to live your life. Who needs 'em? I'm like you, a loner for life."

"Well, I'm glad I wasn't alone today because you saved my life, Corben." Sadie wraps her furry little paws around Corben's feathery neck. She nestles in beside him and they sit together in silence as the sun sets. Corben's eyes start to feel heavy with the weight of the day. Sadie yawns widely.

"I have to get home to my nest, Corben. Please come see me again sometime. You're always welcome in squirrel world." She blows him a little kiss and then scurries away, disappearing into the tree canopy.

In the distance, Corben can see the crow commute heading home. The birds fly together, diving and soaring as one unit. Corben ruffles his feathers and wraps his wings around his body. There is a tear in his eye.

"Loner for life," he says, but no one is around to hear him.

Across the bay, Carlos looks weary as he flies between the commuting crows. "Excuse me?" he says to a fellow commuter in a hoarse, raspy voice. "Have you seen a young crow with a white tail feather?" The crow commuter shakes his head.

Carlos's weariness overtakes him. He lands on a power line and surveys the commuting crowd. After a few moments, he spots a particular crow and his eyes light up. He jumps off the line and flies over to him.

"Henry, have you seen my boy?" he asks. "He hasn't been home since two nights ago."

Henry shakes his head and sighs. "What have they done now?" he asks. "I keep telling those boys to behave themselves, but they just won't listen. Russell and Cameron are like wild animals."

"Will you check with your boys?" Carlos pleads.

"Oh, I'll check with them alright. Lousy good-for-nothin'… They take after their mother's side, you know," says Henry. His feathers puff out as he gets himself worked up.

"Thanks, Henry!" says Carlos and flies off. He becomes just another speck among the thousands of noisy crows darkening the sky. He calls out his son's name over and over again, but his calls go unanswered and fly away on the wind.

CHAPTER 9
RITA'S RABBITS

Morning breaks with a blood-curdling *SCREECH!* Corben jolts awake, nearly falling off the branch. His talons cling to the bark and he pulls himself up, surveying the air around him.

Edgar? he wonders. He hops to the edge of the branch and looks around, but all he sees is a tiny songbird flitting between the trees in search of breakfast.

He hears a seagull call out over the water, and he smiles to himself and relaxes. But then Corben feels the branch bow down under the weight of something that has landed behind him. He freezes. He turns around slowly.

"Boo!" whispers Edgar.

Corben squawks and leaps into the air. Edgar follows, just inches away, so close that he is able to pluck a single feather from Corben's tail. Corben flaps his wings as hard as he can, trying to escape. He flies out over the water, searching for safety on the other side, but all he can see is an empty beach.

Corben dips and dives. He tries to dodge his eagle attacker, but Edgar mirrors his every move. Then Corben spies a kayaker paddling through the early morning waves. He swoops down and lands as softly as he can on the kayak's stern. The kayaker paddles calmly towards the shore, unaware of his stowaway.

Corben hears Edgar let out a frustrated *screech*.

"This isn't over!" Edgar calls. He flaps his strong wings and flies off towards the distant mountains.

The kayak comes to rest on the sandy beach with a *crunch* and the paddler jumps out of the cockpit. He wades through the knee-deep waves and yanks the kayak out of the water.

While the paddler's back is turned, Corben jumps onto the sand, takes a quick look around, and hops down the beach. The waves nip at his talons and he jumps sideways in surprise. He smiles and hops back into the path of the lapping foam, letting it wash over his feet.

Corben's stomach grumbles loudly. It's time for breakfast. A few feet away, a tiny crab shell has washed up on the beach. Corben struts over to check it out and grabs the shell with his beak.

"Hiyah!" says the crab, still very full of life. The crab bursts out of his shell and takes up a kung fu stance with his pincers held up in the air. He snaps his claws, trying to scare the big bad crow. "I am not food!"

Corben throws up his wings in surrender. "I don't want any trouble, tiny friend," he says and backs away.

"Yeah, you better run!" shouts the tiny crab.

Corben retreats, giggling to himself. He takes off and hovers over the beach, looking for something to eat. Near a rock outcropping at the edge of the beach, he lands on a partially submerged rock. He studies the water lapping around its edges. After a few moments, he dunks his head into the water and pulls out a shiny clam shell.

Holding the shell in his beak, he bashes it against the rock. Nothing. He tries again. Still nothing. After three more attempts, the shell remains stubbornly closed. Corben feels frustrated and his stomach growls.

"Yes, I hear you," he says, and then he has a great idea.

Corben hovers high up in the air above the paved parking lot next to the beach. He lets go of the shell and it drops onto the hard concrete. No luck. He flies down to retrieve the shell and then climbs higher into the air. He releases the shell again. Still no luck. Once more, Corben scoops up the shell in his beak and climbs to an even higher height.

Just as he lets go of the shell, a large white rabbit with brown polka-dot patches dashes out from beneath a bush near the parking lot and runs directly into the path of the falling clam shell.

"Watch out!" yells Corben.

The shell smashes on the pavement next to the rabbit and breaks open. The rabbit freezes and then thumps her foot on the ground. Corben zooms down to the ground to claim his clammy prize. Paying no attention to the stamping rabbit, he picks out the fleshy white meat.

The rabbit finally exhales and scolds Corben. "Young man, you must be more careful where you drop things. You could have hurt one of my sweet little ones," she says. She looks over at the nearby bush and calls out. "It's alright, kits, you can come out now."

One by one, tiny bunnies emerge from under the bush. With a big smile on her face, the mama rabbit surveys her multicoloured kits as they hop past her. She points at each bunny in turn, counting them with her paw.

"Lily, Lucy, Lionel, Elsa, Elliott, Edward, Buttons, Snowdrop, Bun Bun, Franklin, FouFou, Chester, Hopper, Pierre…" As the final bunny hops out, a look of confusion washes over her face. Then her expression turns to panic.

"Where's Dash?" she yelps. She hops over to the bush and roots around with her stubby paws, trying to break through the maze of undergrowth. A faint voice can be heard, deep inside the tangled bush.

"I'm stuck!" says the little voice.

Corben can see the panicked scene unfolding as he finishes his meal. He sighs and hops over, popping his head under the bush. He spies the little bunny and sees that his foot is caught in a snarl of spindly branches. Corben snips at the branches with his beak, cutting free the tiny rabbit.

Dash hops out from under the bush and into his mother's paws. She cuddles him close. "Oh, my love, I don't know what I would have done if I'd lost you," she says.

Corben backs out from underneath the bush and stands up tall. When he turns around, a wall of fluff is standing behind him, clapping enthusiastically. He is surrounded by the bunny bunch, all speaking at once.

"That was awesome!" says FouFou.

"You saved him," says Bun Bun.

"Mom, can we keep him?" asks Buttons.

"We'll feed him and give him water every day," says Franklin.

"And take him for walks," says Lionel.

"I don't think crows need to be taken for walks, Lionel. He's not a pet, my loves." She turns to face Corben. "But he is ever so brave." She gives Corben a big fluffy bunny hug. "I'm Rita and this is my family."

"Could he at least come to the beach with us?" asks Dash.

"Well, I suppose he … I didn't catch your name," says Rita.

"I'm Corben." He looks around at the bunnies. "I'd be up for a day at the beach," he says with a smile.

CHAPTER 10
DANGER OVERHEAD

On a secluded part of Jericho Beach, Rita's family and Corben are having a lovely day. At one end of the beach, Edward and Elliott are working together to build a sandcastle. Elliott is hunched over with his back to the castle, scraping sand behind him with his tiny paws. The sand lands in a pile ready to be shaped by Edward, who is moulding it into lopsided towers surrounded by a watery moat. The tower is finished for only a minute before Snowdrop runs towards her brothers, threatening to topple their castle. Edward tackles her before she can reach the moat and they roll around playfully in the sand.

Close by, Franklin is standing next to a bump in the sand with two little black ears sticking out of it. A puff of sand shoots into the sky where a mouth should be and Buttons bursts out of the sand. He takes a deep breath.

"That was the longest yet!" says Franklin. Buttons nods and then lies back down in the sand.

"Again," says Buttons, and Franklin starts shoveling sand over his brother once more.

DANGER OVERHEAD

Not too far away, Elsa, Bun Bun, FouFou, Hopper, Chester, and Pierre are lying face up in the sand with their eyes closed, soaking up the sun.

"Roll!" yells Elsa and they roll over onto their fronts. Their white puffy tails stick up like six cotton balls in a row.

Down at the water's edge, Dash frolics in the frothy foam, hopping up and down and splashing, giggling to himself.

Close by, Rita keeps a watchful eye on her children. She notices Dash and stands up on her hind legs. "Not too far in, Dash. Stay where I can see you," she calls, and then settles back into the sand.

"I'll make sure he doesn't wander too far," says Corben and hops over to Dash. Together they splash around in the shallow water at the edge of the beach. They are having so much fun that they don't notice the menacing presence circling above them.

It happens in an instant. There is a great *screech* and they feel the rush of air as Edgar swoops down and grabs Dash.

"No!" screams Rita.

Edgar looks back and catches Corben's eye. With a devilish grin on his face, he winks. In a flash of black feathers, Corben is airborne.

Little Dash's cries for help can barely be heard over the whooshing wind as Corben climbs through the atmosphere, pumping his wings with all of his might. Edgar glances over his shoulder and grins at Corben, taunting him. He slows his climb to allow Corben to believe he has a chance to catch him, but when Corben gets close, Edgar gives a great flap of his giant wings and pulls away.

DANGER OVERHEAD

Corben doesn't give up. He continues to climb. Suddenly a harbour plane appears out of the clouds. It's heading straight for Edgar, but he doesn't notice because his head is turned, watching Corben. At the last moment, the engine roars and Edgar veers away, narrowly missing the wing of the plane.

The distraction of the plane gives Corben an edge and he catches up with Edgar. He slams the full weight of his body into the eagle's side. Edgar is surprised by the attack and it takes a moment for him to right himself in the sky. When he does, Corben is there, right behind him. Edgar eyes the beach ahead and hatches an evil plan. He flies towards the land and when he gets there, he stops and hovers over the parking lot next to the sand.

"You want him?" Edgar screeches and then laughs his terrifying laugh. "Go get him." Edgar lets go of Dash and the little ball of fur hurtles toward the ground. Rita's screams can be heard from the beach.

Corben plasters his wings to his sides and like a rocket, he shoots towards the pavement. He can see the fear in Dash's eyes as he falls, his little paws scrabbling in the air. At the last second, Corben snatches Dash with his talons. With all his might, he lifts the little bunny into the air and flies towards the rabbit family on the beach. He places Dash gently onto the ground at Rita's feet and she scoops him up in her paws.

Corben collapses on the sand, completely exhausted. But there is no time to catch his breath. The sky goes dark above him and he hears Edgar's maniacal laugh. The rabbits freeze in place, too terrified to scream, as Edgar lands a few feet away from Corben.

Corben has nothing left, but somehow he manages to get to his feet. He stands tall between the eagle and the rabbits. He lunges at Edgar with a mighty *CAW* and then they are in the sky once more. Corben attacks with his beak and then his talons, alternating in an all-out assault on the eagle. Edgar responds and rips out a chunk of feathers from Corben's chest.

The two birds lock their talons together and cartwheel towards the ground in a deathly spiral. Just before they slam into the ocean below, they disengage their talons and race back up into the air. As the battle rages, they make their way inland towards the forest.

Hovering above the tree canopy, Edgar grabs hold of Corben's wing in his powerful yellow beak and there is a loud *CRUNCH* and a *CRACK*. Corben screams in pain and his wing goes limp by his side. He flails with his other wing but he can't keep himself airborne. Corben crashes through the trees. He slams into the ground and the world goes dark.

CHAPTER 11
A VOICE IN THE SKY

Sometime later, Corben wakes up with a jolt and cries out in pain. He cradles his wing and falls back into the underbrush. The shadows are long in the dense forest. Dark clouds have gathered in the sky. *CRACK!* The sky lights up, followed by a rumbling wave of thunder. Corben shudders and tears run down his beak.

Then he hears a faint voice in the darkness. At first he thinks he is imagining the voice. He can barely hear it over the thunder.

"Corben ... Corben...," the voice calls.

Corben thinks he must be dreaming. It couldn't possibly be who he thinks it is, but he knows that voice.

"Dad?" he croaks, barely able to make a sound. There is no reply.

"Please don't go," pleads Corben. He tries to stand but it's a struggle. He uses his good wing to push himself up, but he winces from the pain in his broken wing. He takes one step. Then another. He manages a hop. Then another. With great effort he hops to the base of a towering Sitka spruce.

Corben takes a deep breath and grabs hold of the bark with one talon. His injured wing hangs by his side. Remembering how he raced Sadie, he latches onto the trunk with his beak and alternates his feet, sinking his talons into the bark, one after the other. Slowly, he claws his way up the tree. The effort exhausts him but he keeps going.

A VOICE IN THE SKY

There is another *crack* of lightning and a thunderous shake and the rain comes. It pounds against Corben, soaking him as he climbs.

"I'm coming … Dad … please don't go." He reaches the canopy and the sky opens up above him. He uses the last of his strength to yell into the night. "Dad!"

A shadowy figure appears. Corben breathes a sigh of relief, but then he realizes that the shadow isn't a crow. It's an eagle. And it lands next to Corben.

"Poor, pathetic crow. All alone," sneers Edgar. "It almost feels too easy." He extends his giant wings and lets out a piercing *screech* as a great clap of thunder booms.

Corben closes his eyes, waiting for the end. But the strike doesn't come. Corben opens his eyes and sees Carlos standing defiantly between him and Edgar. His wings are extended, shielding his son.

"He is NOT alone," booms Carlos and the sky fills with hundreds of crows, their chorus of caws echoing above the thunder.

Edgar's scowl turns to a look of fear as the crows surround him. He stumbles in retreat, his wings flailing as he tries to take flight. The crows chase him into the night.

Carlos turns to face his son and Corben collapses into his father's outstretched wings.

A VOICE IN THE SKY

Corben wakes up to find his mother next to him, cradling his head with her wing. He realizes that he is home. Soon Sheryl is pushed aside by Corben's tiny siblings, who are suddenly all over him, a bundle of feathers and excitement.

"Is he awake?!" they cheep in unison.

"Gentle, darlings, gentle. Your brother is hurt," says Sheryl. Corben looks down and sees that his broken wing has been tied in a sling made of leaves and vines. His little brother holds up his own injured wing, tied in a similar, much smaller sling.

"Samesies!" says the little chick.

"It's a pretty nasty break, but Doc Crow thinks it will heal in a few weeks," says Sheryl. She wraps one wing around the little chick and pulls Corben close with the other. Corben closes his eyes and leans into his mom's embrace, feeling the comfort of it. But soon he pulls back. He feels embarrassed and he lowers his head.

"Mom … I'm … I'm really sorry for everything," he says and takes a deep breath. "I should never have left the chicks alone. I'm so sorry for all the things I said."

"Oh, my love, what matters is you're okay and we're all together."

"Not all of us," says Corben and he looks up at his mother. "Where's Dad? Do you think he will ever forgive me?"

"Corben, your father loves you very much. He always has and always will. He just has a hard time showing it. He works so hard to keep everyone safe and it weighs on him." Sheryl gives Corben a squeeze with her wing. "But he didn't move from your side all night. He wanted to be here when you woke up, but…" Sheryl pauses. She doesn't know whether or not she should tell Corben the truth.

"Mom? What is it?" asks Corben.

"It's happened, love. What we feared. The humans came with their big machines. Henry and his family lost their tree."

"What?! They cut it down? Are Russ and Cam okay?"

"Yes, don't worry, they weren't hurt. They're staying with Henry's cousin. We couldn't wait any longer. Your Dad called an emergency meeting this morning."

"What are we waiting for then? We should be there!" cries Corben. He struggles to stand up, wincing from the pain in his wing.

"Corben, dear, you need to rest."

"No, Mom. I need to help."

The Gathering Oak is filled with hundreds of silent crows. Sheryl and Corben land among them, arriving just in time to see Carlos step forward to address the community.

"My fellow crows, you have always put your faith in me. It has been an honour and a privilege to lead you, but today, I do not bring you the news you deserve. I have failed you. I have not been able to save our home. I am also sad to report that we have not found a new roost that could accommodate everyone. I am afraid that means our community won't be able to stay together."

Corben looks at his mother and she drops her head as a tear falls from her eye.

"This, my friends, is our darkest hour," says Carlos. "The great metal beasts are here. We have to go."

"But Mr. Mayor, where *can* we go?" asks a crow in the crowd.

Off in the distance, the wail of a seagull can be heard. The sound pulls Corben's attention away from the meeting.

"Wait!" Corben hops forward. He stands on the edge of the branch and calls to his father. "Mr. Mayor?" he says and then clears his throat. "Dad?"

The crowd falls silent. Carlos looks up into the tree and is surprised to see his son.

"I have an idea," says Corben.

CHAPTER 12
A NEW LIFE

A lone crow walks through a dark tunnel. He sees only a small glow of light ahead. The light becomes brighter and brighter until the crow emerges into a spectacular grove. He stops at the entrance to the grove and drops his two little suitcases with a *thud*. He stares at the grove in awe. Behind him, a wave of crows emerges one by one from the tunnel, carrying everything they own. They look nervous and tired, but there is a glimmer of hope in their eyes.

A giant seagull appears in front of them, like a glittering mirage. "Welcome to Steven's Grove, my friends. *My home*, as they say, *is your home*. I invite you to choose a tree and make yourselves comfy." Steven motions to the grove with a great sweep of his large white wing.

Corben is perched in a tree nearby, watching as the crows enter the grove. He spots his best friends and smiles. Russell looks up into the tree and notices Corben. He elbows Cameron, who looks in Corben's direction as well. The brothers nod at their friend and each give him two wing-tips-up. Corben bows to them, grinning broadly.

A NEW LIFE

Carlos lands next to his son and wraps his wing around Corben. He surveys the community in their new home. "You've done well, son."

"Thanks, Dad."

"I'm so proud of the crow you've become," says Carlos. "Because of you, the community can stay together. I think you'll make a great leader when the time comes."

Corben looks uncomfortable. "Dad, I wanted to help but being mayor is your thing. It's not mine." He pauses and lowers his head. "I'm sorry to disappoint you again."

"Hey now, don't say that. I've been hard on you and I'm sorry. If you feel that community service isn't for you, I understand."

"That's not it," says Corben. "I wanna help, but I just think there's a different way I can do it. A way that's more me."

"Well, alright then. What do you have in mind?"

Five crows stand in a line on a branch, bouncing with nervous energy and clicking away to each other. Across from them, Corben stands before a banner made of ragged cloth, with sticks that spell out "Corben's Adventure School."

"Ready for some fun?" Corben yells.

The young crows respond all together with a loud yes.

"Oh, come on. You can do better than that! I said, are you ready for some fun?!" Corben yells again.

A NEW LIFE

"YES!" the crows shout, even louder this time.

"That's better! Let's go!"

The group follows Corben through the old-growth forest of Stanley Park. They dip and dive between the extended branches, feeling the wind in their wings.

Out of the corner of his eye, Corben notices a rustling on a branch. He smiles to himself as Sadie bursts from the tangle of branches and flies through the air. She lands on a branch for a second, just long enough for Corben to notice a cheeky wink before she is off again, bounding from tree to tree. Corben takes chase, with the adventuring crows following close behind.

It's showtime at the aquarium. There is a moment of calm and then a shiny grey dolphin breaks the surface of the water and jumps into the air. She is suspended in midair for a moment before falling back into the water, sending a wave splashing over the crowd. Today the crowd includes six captivated crows and a very excited squirrel clapping their wings and paws together.

On the far side of the aquarium, Bill is enjoying a hot dog with all the toppings. He notices something strange. Are those crows clapping? he wonders. He looks again but this time all he sees is a handful of crows perched on the fence, acting pretty crow-like. He shakes his head and takes another squishy bite of his hot dog. A line of bright red ketchup oozes down the front of his uniform.

It's lunchtime for the delighted crows. Corben demonstrates his now-perfected food-stealing technique on an unsuspecting little boy standing near the water at Granville Island. As the boy munches on a piece of pizza, the sun glints off the gooey goodness of the cheese.

The student crows look on from under a nearby bench as Corben creeps towards his prize. He looks back at the group to make sure they

A NEW LIFE

are paying close attention. They nod in reply as he demonstrates his sneaky approach. And then, he CAWS—a blaring, startling sound, which is followed by a scream and a *splat*.

Lunch is served.

Later, the crows stand on the beach with their talons in the surf. Corben demonstrates how to find the tastiest clams under the water. While his students explore with their beaks, Corben looks around and spies Rita on the far side of the beach. In an instant, Dash is by her side, waving his little paw in the air to greet his hero. Corben waves back and then turns his attention to his students.

At the end of the day, Corben and his students join the crow commute back to the grove. The commute doesn't feel like a chore anymore. Corben looks forward to these daily flights with his friends. He loves his new life.

In the orange glow just before twilight, Corben stands next to his father, perched at the very top of the Lions Gate Bridge. To the east, the city towers sparkle gold and yellow from the sun's last rays.

"You ready?" Corben asks.

"I think it's about time I had some fun," replies Carlos and he nods to Corben. "I'm ready."

Father and son leap into the air together. Their ecstatic cries echo through the evening calm. Just as they are about to splash into the surf, they pull up and sail on the wind above the salty waves. They soar side by side towards the setting sun.

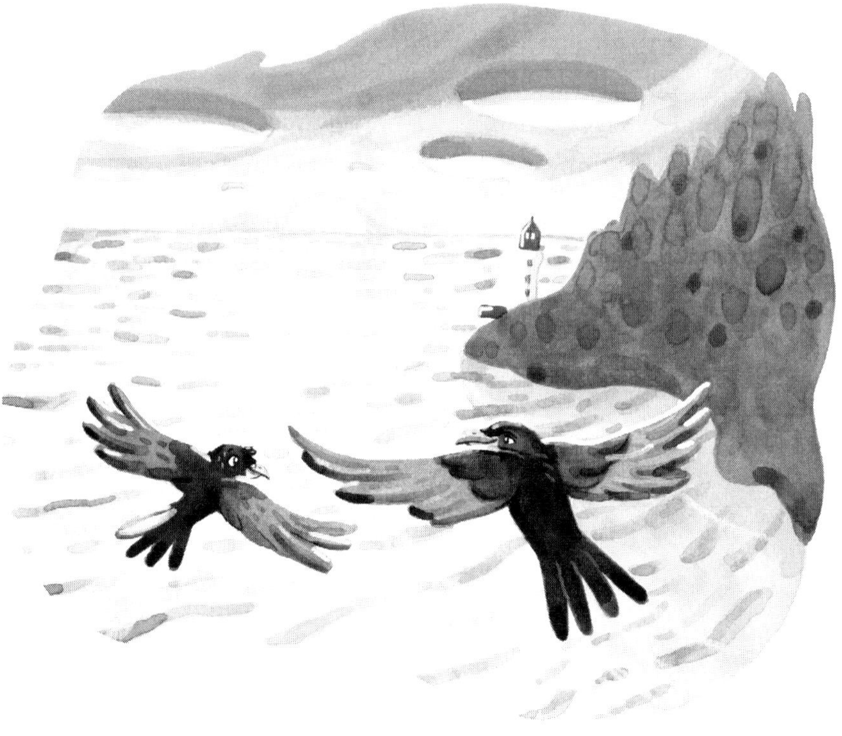

The Real Crow Commute

This story was inspired by a real crow commute. Since the early 1970s, thousands of crows have commuted from their roost in Burnaby to Vancouver every day, like clockwork. In the spring and the fall, my own commute coincides with that of the crows. Sometimes I find my commute quite boring. One day, I wondered if any of the crows felt the same way. That was the day Corben hatched in my mind.

We all know crows can't actually talk, but a lot of the animal behaviours in this story are real. Crows are intelligent, inventive, and loyal. They don't go to school with Professor Pluma, but they do use twigs as tools. There may not be a Mayor Crow holding meetings in the Gathering Oak, but crows are sociable birds and they are protective of their families. They mate for life and the younger crows help raise new chicks. When they are threatened, crows come together to protect each other.

We share our cities with so many different creatures, and each one has its own fascinating story to tell. I encourage you to look around and learn about the animals and birds that live where you live. Maybe they will inspire you to write your own story.

EMILY LONIE was born in Ottawa but now calls Vancouver home, where she appreciates all the natural beauty the city has to offer. *Corben and the Crow Commute* is her first novel.

Manufactured by Amazon.ca
Acheson, AB